Balancing Act

poems by

Terry Persun

Cyberwit.net
HIG 45 Kaushambi Kunj, Kalindipuram
Allahabad - 211011 (U.P.) India
http://www.cyberwit.net
Tel: +(91) 9415091004 +(91) (532) 2552257
E-mail: info@cyberwit.net

Printed at Thomson Press India Limited.

For Catherine

Acknowledgements:

A Philosophy or Sunlight – *Blue Unicorn*

How Great the Silence – *Dandelion Soul* (chapbook collection)

It's Personal – *Steam Ticket*

Progress – *And Now This* (collection)

The River Man – *Barn Tarot* (collection) and *Every Leaf* (collection)

Weeds – *Blue Unicorn*

Without Pain – *Wind* and *Every Leaf* (collection)

Statement

Short poems seem to be the most difficult to write. They are also the ones that appear to weigh the most, have the most baggage and back-story that is untold but present in the silences. In these short poems, collected over many years, I've tried to find a path through to a story.

After culling through four or five times more poems than are presented here, I began to see a pattern building. A beginning, middle, and end that could be pieced together. Once the pattern made itself clear to me—and perhaps only me—I nonetheless pulled the poems together into nine stories that also had their own overarching story.

This is where discretion and planning came in. From the nine stories another pattern emerged, which I chose to follow throughout this work. That pattern was a sequence that had a beginning poem, three middle poems, and an end poem. This meant culling through more poems, shortening the longer stories, and taking the chance that my cutting of poems might cause a longer story to lose its way, become more abstract. Yet, I realized that such a thing isn't always bad. It might open a wider window for the reader to insert herself.

Once I had the stories complete, it was time to title them. Each group of five poems has its own title; my hope to string the pieces together one last time. The book's title connotes the balancing act of life that we all must face and maneuver. In the end, I give these poems away as every poet must do, for readers must follow their own paths through these poems and find their own way home.

—Terry Persun

Contents

Opening Up

Shadorma Duo: Finding

I

Beginning
with only true love
we enter
the good life
finding that our own child's birth
brought us together.

II

The old oak
lifts high above me.
New leaves of
yellow spring
promise to become wilder
with the sound of birds.

What Morning Brings

I want the scent and sound of morning:
the rock ledge accented
by green, brown, and gray light
smelling like olives
and fresh fruit lying in dirt.

The clear sound of leaves
clack together in tight air.
Invisible birds communicate
in ways I don't understand.
There is a psychic connection here,

too loose to explain
in the block letters
of words and language,
too wild to let go of
in this easy morning.

Dialog of the Great Spirit

There is something beyond *me*, too.
I know its weight.
Its purpose unfolds through me.
Yet, I also know
that I am all things—even that.

Trees in Spring

Trees lay their blossoms down
to hide the gray-sad sidewalk
from those walking alone.
As the blossoms brown
and blow away, spring tumbles
forward toward summer heat
and long, lazy green days.

Rock Thoughts

The sound of creek rocks
lifts from the bed
like forgotten water
heading toward the skinny faucet
in my simple home.
I drink their memories
and turn them into poems.

Arriving Late

Announcement

Something slips under
the carpet of wind
and hides.

I wonder about leaves
and the secrets they hold
in their hands.

Before sun breaks
through cracks in clouds, the rain
announces its arrival.

Shadows

Even at night shadows shift
and turn
along the path.

There is always
a glimmer of light:
perhaps a car traveling
over the mountain pass

or someone
with a bright lantern
walking alone
in the dark woods.

Bashful Moon

Hiding among tree branches
the shy moon moves
heavily into the night sky
a step at a time.

approaching rain clouds
coyote's
gray eyes

Last Walk

One last march
around the neighborhood
before the mountain
swallows the sun whole
and leaves me walking
through the coolness
of a lovely summer evening.

Growing Together

It's Personal

The turkey vulture sits
atop the fence post,
its wings spread
in arrogant display,

its natural leanings
toward personal preference,
an arrogance I am trying
to allow back into my life.

Moon

I am afraid of the moon,
its string of light falling
and pooling on the ground
like water from a glass.

Grapes

Dad had one vine
for wine
then elderberry
in season
and dandelion.

Outside

I find
the conversation
of gnats
more comforting
than television.

This Child's Wish

Cradle me in arms of trees
and flesh of bears.

Allow the cold waters of pain
to swallow me whole.

Stuff me and bloat me
with more than my fill.

Darkness Enters

Afternoon Light

The leaves of maples juggle
sunlight amid shadow. Dark

trunks scream, penetrate the folly
of leaves, try to catch the luminous light

that evades their shadowy fingers,
their dark thoughts.

Birds Know

The birds know the universe
was made from nothing
more than the thoughts
of every living thing,

and are not afraid, like humans,
who don't understand
that it's one big mistake
of one small mystery.

Night

When the sun pulls
the dark from the ground
and lifts it into the sky,
fireflies become stars,
my soul the dark matter
between them.

Moth

Like a guard,
if performs
its appointed
rounds
outside my window,
keeping out
the darkness.

Snow

Snow floats into the net
like fluffed rain
from a shivering pine branch.

The swell of wind matches
that of the deer's chest.

A rifle cracks and snaps
the deer's breath short.

Wind shakes snow
from the innocent pine,
splattered with warm blood.

Shifts and Turns

Balance

The shadow of trees
lightly touches the brown grass
and shifts in the slow wind.
The guard rail's
hard-edged shadow,
like a heavy black line,
does not move.
The boy bends
to touch the darkness
just as he lifts his face
to the warmth of the sun.

Pulling Back

Sticks, like sailboats, drift
over the pond's surface

in bright sunlight, in spring.
The bright-eyed fish

search for food at the water's edge
every time an insect connects,

every time a small boy spits.
When the turtles rise up

and climb to the tops of rocks,
it is time to pull back into the woods

and dream of an earlier life
when the sun didn't feel so hot.

God Stares at His Image in the Mirror

There is something about the Earth
that makes me love her.
The gentle breeze,
the powerful ocean,
our wild and mixed children.

barbed wire fence
    tightrope
        for hanging roses

Worms

On rainy days, worms
believe they can
make it across the desert
of sidewalk,
where I find them
dried in sudden sun.

One Change

A Change Comes

Overlook one hello or birthday,
swerve away from a wayward squirrel,
refuse to make eye contact, and change
occurs like a snake bite on a hot day.

What accident of life might be missed
several miles down the road?
What person might you run into
who ends up being your spouse?

A storm rolls over the mountain
like an avalanche. One choice,
to run or to face it, can alter your life.
There is no understanding in weather.

Buck

A ten-pointer stares
into my passenger
side window as though we know
each other.
I drive past slowly
allowing the present moment
to slip between
our fading memories.

Dolly

One of the horses is mine
but I had to get married
at seventeen
and missed
our entire life together.

moonrise
    water shifts
        its weight

Shadorma Duo: Losing

I

A country
farm, supposed to be
our savior
extended
our finances and lives too
far to recover.

II

The water
floods the shallow creek
banks with melt
from winter
snows and then kills everything
that gets in the way.

Growing Apart

Apart

Two branches join
at the source
for a conversation
about life
and why soon
they will grow
apart.

In Winter

The quiet snow has fallen
over the lake and the trees
like understanding enters
a conversation about love.
In the pure white,
adrenaline flows like anger
slowed to a calming speed.

The wind in the woods
is still. No words are spoken
out of turn, yet no emotions
are left untouched.

An Unnatural Path

Through the openings between trees
in the forest, there is an unnatural path
which leads to a wide pond
placed at the edge of a hay field

near a wood frame house and barn.
The flat black of water reflects
a bird infested sky.

Near the edge, the pond scum separates
and the silver bellies of minnows wink.
Tadpoles slip near the green of a stem
and dream of having legs.

How Great the Silence

Against the dark sky
blackened trees stand
leading to a void.
Strands of branches,
like cracked glass
shatter the sky
into just air.

Sleeping a winter's hibernation
until the spring of a new day,
nothing stirs and nothing notices
how great the silence,
how surreal the planet.

Progress

They fixed the highway
near Old Oak Road

Now, when you reach the ridge

on Bastion's Hill
you can't see the old oak.

Overcoming Obstacles

Weeds

I step over weeds
growing between sidewalk
cracks as not to damage
their fragile bodies
which have worked
so hard to find their way
into the light.

Lily Pad

Floating on water's surface tension,
an island for insects,
frogs and raindrops, green,
shaped like a rounded heart,
who would know
that its anchor is a long stem,
diving deeply into the black,
black water for nourishment?
Its flower, during the right season,
is its only show of a life
with any beauty.

owl call
    horses race
        to the far field

Dark Night

The coyotes cry
like children, happy
to find food
in their once empty bowls.

The River Man

At night, the river is black.
Black coal.
He swings
from a rope tied
to the black branch
of a dark, dark oak.

Hitting the black water,
the cold water,
he swims down
toward the back
of his heart
looking for light.

Surviving

Corn

In rows, was how I once lived.
Too tall to see over,
too green to hide in woods.

Rowed like boats
in single file,
one beside another,

driving toward the horizon
as though there were no end.

A Philosophy of Sunlight

It hardly matters
that the sun fades
in and out from cloudcover,
shyly winking shadows
across the sidewalk
knowing that light
is all we have.

Without Pain

All the pink and yellow flowers
slip into night like frogs slip
into the thin scum of a pond.

Color recedes and petals fold
into themselves. The flowers hide.
There are no bees to torment them.

This Far

Having walked this far,
sure no time has passed,
I no longer feel youthful.

Yet time dances as it always has.

The sky remains a close friend,
rain, a meaning I can't touch.
Trees continue to know my name.

Full

The moon, like a solar lamp,
dim and magical, lights
the fence row
coming down the lane
from feeding the horses
their last meal of the evening.